I0805962

TOP DOG Breeds

LABRADOR RETRIEVERS

Christina Earley

Table of Contents

A Starfish Book

SEAHORSE PUBLISHING

Teaching Tips for Caregivers:

As a caregiver, you can help your child succeed in school by giving them a strong foundation in language and literacy skills and a desire to learn to read.

This book helps children grow by letting them practice reading skills.

Reading for pleasure and interest will help your child develop reading skills and will give your child the opportunity to practice these skills in meaningful ways.

- Encourage your child to read on their own at home.
- Encourage your child to practice reading aloud.
- Encourage activities that require reading.
- Establish a reading time.
- Talk with your child.
- Give your child writing materials.

Teaching Tips for Teachers:

Research shows that one of the best ways for students to learn a new topic is to read about it.

Before Reading

- Read the "Words to Know" and discuss the meaning of each word.
- Read the back cover to see what the book is about.

During Reading

- When a student gets to a word that is unknown, ask them to look at the rest of the sentence to find clues to help with the meaning of the unknown word.
- Ask the student to write down any pages of the book that were confusing to them.

After Reading

- Discuss the main idea of the book.
- Ask students to give one detail that they learned from the book by showing a text-dependent answer from the book.

Labrador Retrievers

Woof! Woof!

Labrador retrievers are **popular** pets.

Labrador retrievers are often called Labs.

Labs are medium-sized dogs.

They have wide heads with **floppy** ears.

Fun Fact

Lab colors can be black, chocolate, or yellow.

Labs are sporting dogs.

They find and bring back small animals.

Fun Fact

The word *retrieve* means "to find and bring back."

Labs have a **waterproof** coat.

Webbed paws help them swim.

Labs can run very fast.

They love to play.

Labrador retrievers are smart.

They like to learn new tricks.

Fun Fact

Labrador retrievers are easy to train.

Labs need two meals a day.

Brushing them daily gets out loose hair.

Fun Fact

Labrador retrievers shed a lot.

Labs are friendly to everyone.

They do not make good **watchdogs**!

Some Labs have jobs as guide dogs.

Others are search and rescue dogs.

Quiz: Am I Ready for a Dog?

Find out if you are ready to own a dog.

Answer *yes* or *no* for each question.

1. I will help with feeding.
2. I will scoop poop.
3. I will help with training.
4. I will help with exercise.
5. I will be okay if some of my things get ruined.

Scoring:

Give yourself one point for each *yes* answer. Then, count up your total.

4 to 5: You are ready to talk to your caregivers about getting a dog.

2 to 3: You are not quite ready yet. Maybe next year.

0 to 1: You are not ready at all.

Staying Safe Around Dogs

DO	DO NOT
✓ Ask permission to pet a dog.	✗ Run up to a dog.
✓ Let the dog sniff your closed hand before petting.	✗ Bark or growl at a dog.
✓ Leave a dog alone when it is eating and sleeping.	✗ Ride or sit on a dog.
✓ Notice and listen to a dog's body language.	✗ Pull a dog's ears or tail.
✓ Respect a dog's space.	✗ Tease a dog.

Words to Know

floppy (FLAH-pee): tending to flop or bend over

popular (PAHP-yuh-lur): liked by many

watchdogs (WAHCH-dawgs): dogs kept to guard property

waterproof (WAW-tur-proof): protected from letting water in and getting soaked

webbed (webd): having the toes connected by skin

Index

Comprehension Questions

1. A Labrador retriever is a ______ dog.
   a. running
   b. sporting
   c. herding

2. Labrador retrievers have _____ paws.
   a. webbed b. wet c. soft

3. How many times should you feed a Lab each day?
   a. once
   b. three times
   c. twice

4. **True or False:** Labrador retrievers are good watchdogs.

5. **True or False:** Labrador retrievers like to learn new tricks.

Answers
1. b 2. a 3. c 4. False 5. True

About the Author

Christina Earley lives in south Florida with her husband, son, and dog Bailey. When she is not writing books, she visits her local Humane Society to play with the dogs, cats, and bunnies. She likes to hike in the mountains and bake chocolate chip cookies.

Written by: Christina Earley
Design by: Kathy Walsh
Editor: Kim Thompson

Library of Congress PCN Data
Labrador Retrievers / Christina Earley
Top Dog Breeds
ISBN 979-8-8873-5943-4 (hard cover)
ISBN 979-8-8873-5982-3 (paperback)
ISBN 979-8-8904-2041-1 (EPUB)
ISBN 979-8-8904-2100-5 (eBook)
Library of Congress Control Number: 2023913162

Printed in the United States of America.

Photographs/Shutterstock: Cover & Title pg: grafienver_icons_logo, Ivanna-Ivashka, pnDl, provector, higedanddy, Eric Isselee; pg numbers: Alemon cz; Fun Facts p 4, 13, 17: Elena Pimukova; p 21: Chief Design; p 3, 5, 7, 9, 11, 13, 15, 17, 19 Ivanna_Ivashka; p 3: MirasWonderland; p 5: Rosa Jay, Natalia Fedosova; p 6, 7: Anna Pozzi - Zoophotos; p 8: otsphoto; p 9: Annette Shaff; p 10: anetapics; p 11: GoDog Photo; p 12: Julian Popov; p 13: Mark Herreid; p 14: Pixel-Shot; p 15: Olga Ilina; p 16: manushot; p 17: Prostock-studio; p 18: Africa Studio; p 19: Vladimir Staykov; p 21: antoniodiaz

Seahorse Publishing Company
www.seahorsepub.com

Copyright © 2025 **SEAHORSE PUBLISHING COMPANY**

All rights reserved. No part of this publication may be reproduced, stored in a retrieval system or be transmitted in any form or by any means, electronic, mechanical, photocopying, recording, or otherwise, without the prior written permission of Seahorse Publishing Company.

Published in the United States
Seahorse Publishing
PO Box 771325
Coral Springs, FL 33077

SEAHORSE PUBLISHING